Images of the

MEDWAY TOWNS

Images of the
MEDWAY TOWNS

Kent Messenger
Group Newspapers

breedon **books**
PUBLISHING

First published in Great Britain by
The Breedon Books Publishing Company Limited
Breedon House, Unit 3 The Parker Centre, Mansfield Road, Derby
DE21 4SZ, 1996

Acknowledgements

The preparation of this book has benefited greatly from several
publications edited by the late H.R.Pratt Boorman, proprietor and
editor-in-chief of the *Kent Messenger* for many years. They
include *Hell's Corner* (1940), *Kent – Our Glorious Heritage*
(1950), *Kent Unconquered* (1951), *Kent Inns – a Distillation*
(1955), *Kent Messenger Centenary* (1959), *Pictures of Maidstone*
(1965), *Kent A Royal County* (1966), *Spirit of Kent* (1968) and
Kent Our County (1979). Much help has also been received from
members of the photographic department of the *Kent Messenger*,
who took most of the pictures, Kent Messenger Group Central
Information Unit and former staff journalist Roy Plascott.

ISBN 1 85983 386 1

Printed and bound by Butler & Tanner Ltd., Selwood Printing
Works, Caxton Road, Frome, Somerset.

Jackets printed by Lawrence-Allen, Weston-super-Mare, Avon.

Contents

Introduction
6

The Changing Scene in the
Towns and Around
8

Royal Visits, Civic Events, Celebrations
66

People and Events
85

The River Medway, the Dockyard,
Naval and Military
101

The Cathedral, Churches and Pubs
128

The Towns at War
157

Sport and Recreation
181

So Many Stunning Changes
188

Introduction

THE five Medway Towns have finally become one.

Since the publication of the previous edition of *Images of the Medway Towns* the area merged under one unitary authority, Medway Council, in 1998. Although many people in Chatham, Gillingham, Rochester, Strood and Rainham still proudly hold on to their own identity, the unification is seen by many as common sense.

Many in the rest of Kent considers the Medway Towns to be one place, and geographically they are. Like five London boroughs stacked side by side, however distinct and separate in identity, it only takes the crossing of a road or the walking up a street to go though a boundary. Indeed many living within the area find it hard to tell where one town begins and where another ends.

Only a small, barely noticeable sign marked Chatham, as you walk east along Rochester High Street, shows that you have now actually crossed into Chatham High Street. More confusingly, halfway up Chatham Hill you suddenly find yourself in Gillingham, yet a mile or so further on one side of the main road is still Chatham.

And so much of the dockyard was in Gillingham yet it was labelled as belonging to Chatham. At least Strood and the Hoo Peninsula are clearly divided from the rest of the area by the River Medway.

In local authority terms Medway has become a republic within Kent, now totally independent of the county.

As if to further stress the uniqueness of the area, a movement grew to press for city status, particularly with applications made by Medway Council and local newspaper campaigning.

After all it is conurbation with a cathedral, and a population of 250,000, making it the largest urban community in the South-east. To many that is a city in practice.

Some feared the council unification could stifle the individual identity of the towns. But then before 1998 Chatham, Strood and the Hoo Peninsula were swallowed up by a council named after Rochester.

And in any case everyone knows the wide diversity within Medway's boundaries. Certainly the range of wealth and poverty is a immense and paradoxical. Medway has a large population of people in the bottom socio-economic groups and there are many pockets of deprivation – Chatham's Town ward is classed as the second poorest in Kent. Yet just a few miles away are some of the richest wards in the county, such as Hempstead and Wigmore.

The bulk of this book is predominantly concerned with scenes and events in Medway from the 1930s to the 1970s, as shown by the pictures compiled by the original author, John Evans. But there is an entirely new chapter bringing the story right up to the 21st century.

Despite the horrors of the Second World War most things were a good deal more settled in the middle of the 20th century: the key factors of everyday life were established and everyone through they would remain so throughout their lives – schools, workplaces, churches, pubs and so one.

But an entire prop of the area collapsed in

1984 with the closure of the Chatham Dockyard Royal Navy base, causing the wipeout of 8,000 jobs. Suddenly the old certainties vanished but Medway people have proved to be resilient in coping with drastic changes, good or bad.

The 1984 closure has been overcome by a brilliant rebirth of the yard as a tourist attraction and craft centre that makes maximum use of the largest concentration of listed buildings in Britain.

An entirely new community has been built on St Mary's Island at Chatham Maritime, complete with a new primary school to cater for the several hundred young children of families moving into the smart new houses. As part of the rebirth even the Chatham Navy Days were revived in 1999 after an 18-year absence.

Rochester also revitalised itself by capitalising on the advantages of the Charles Dickens connection. Rochester to many in the outside world is considered the most prestigious of the five Medway towns. The castle makes a great impression on the landscape and its companion cathedral even more so as befits its ranking as the second oldest in England after Canterbury. Rochester is simply full of history and makes the most of it, as old as Gillingham is new. Chatham may have a reputation of being rough and ready like so many military and naval towns but it is vibrant and has an excellent shopping area. Kent's most heavily-populated town used to be called, not Gillingham but New Brompton and indeed that was the name of the football club that has put the Towns on the sporting map. Gillingham FC has particularly thrived since the mid-1990s and today stands proudly in the First Division.

Even in recent years it appeared that painful struggles were far from over – the club lost the chance of promotion at Wembley in the cruellest possible way in 1999, through a penalty shootout. Yet it bounced back with a vengeance exactly a year later, winning the play-offs to reach the long craved-for Division One.

Apart from the Priestfield Stadium, Gillingham has a critical shopping nerve centre, Hempstead Valley, attracting people for miles, and the town has always been a fine centre of entertainment, such as with its ice bowl. It also has the assets of light industry and commerce.

Beyond the urban areas the most far-reaching changes in the period under review took place on the vast Hoo Peninsula, which divides the Medway from the mighty Thames. Her agriculture and important wildlife reserves managed to prosper in the shadow of a giant refinery and power station.

To the south what were virtually small industrial towns have had to overcome the loss of traditional business like cement manufacture. Elsewhere there are some extremely attractive villages such as Cooling and Upnor: Medway is by no means all urbanised.

The Towns have lost most of their military connections, which over the years could scarcely have been more important. And crucially much of the prosperity that stemmed from the river has gone – the barges, and, above all, the Shorts flying boats and seaplanes.

Perhaps the Towns were destined never to settle for too long. Visit them after even a couple of years and you find the layout of the roads have changed.

Those who have not travelled into Chatham on the A229 since 1999, for instance, would be completely stunned by the changes around the M2. Those driving to cross the River Medway are confronted by not one motorway bridge but two, and a Channel Tunnel Rail Link bridge running parallel. And, of course, you can now also cross the river underwater, though the Medway Tunnel.

Even aspects of the population are changing. At the time of writing Medway is having a university explosion with the University of Kent at Medway building a brand new campus for about 6,000 students. The combined population of the UKM and the University of Greenwich campus is expected to shortly reach about 10,000.

Who knows what sort of changes Medway will see in the future.?

Chatham in 1970, when many of the important developments had not begun, notably the building of the Pentagon

the Towns and Around

Shopping Centre.

The Town Hall has been a dominant feature of the Chatham scene since it was opened by the Earl of Rosebery in 1900.

The buses struggled on during the severe winter of 1962-63, but there was not much other business in Military Road on this day.

The junction of Railway Street and Maidstone Road, Chatham in the late 1960s. Southern Railway was still running the station, as the sign indicates.

The top end of Chatham High Street in 1969 – now a much-changed area. This picture was probably taken on a Sunday.

Time for peace and quiet at Magpie Hall Road and Coney Banks – a 1950s picture.

Where Rochester joins Chatham in New Road – a view from 1955.

People were getting used to peace in the summer of 1946 – and you really could buy a suit for fifty shillings (£2.50) in Chatham High Street.

This picture (and the two on the next page) show a long lost scene – Chatham High Street during World War Two. The atmosphere of austerity is heightened by a miserably wet day.

Chatham High Street during World War Two.

The staff at Chatham's G.H.Hadaway's store in the 1930s, when a week's supply of groceries was delivered to many homes.

The Hospital of John Hawkins in Chatham in 1956. Hawkins, an officer in Elizabeth I's Navy, founded the original hospital for disabled and poor mariners and shipwrights.

Watts Place, Chatham in 1945, one of many side streets demolished to make way for commercial development. It ran between High Street and Medway Street and became the site of Bates and then Bentalls stores, also now gone. Note the instruction that pedal cycles must be pushed by hand.

Shades of the Steptoes! In 1959 there was still a use for horse troughs, but this one at Luton Arches was already earmarked to go as major road improvements were carried out.

Another view of Luton Arches at the same period. It was one of the Towns' worst traffic blackspots.

All Saints' Hospital, Chatham, in 1971. It was already well-over a hundred years old and a modern replacement had been talked about for a long time. Other hospitals have been built, but All Saints' remains in service.

The Salvation Army band plays carols during its annual visit to All Saints' in 1969.

The Naval War Memorial at Chatham's Great Lines, pictured in 1951.

The Waghorn Memorial in Railway Street. When the statue was originally erected in New Cut in 1888, dedicated to local-born Lt Thomas Waghorn, who opened up the overland route to India, he was seen to be pointing to that country.

The War Memorial in Victoria Gardens.

This dominant Watling Street building suffered from two changing entertainment tastes – it was a cinema and then a bowling centre before being converted to commercial use. This picture was taken in 1969.

The old Empire in Chatham High Street. A famous music hall for many years, it closed in the 1960s. When this picture was taken not long before then, there was also still an adjoining cinema.

A wartime shot of The Ritz cinema in Chatham High Street, one of those which has survived with changes to its ownership and name.

The old Chatham Library in New Road in the late 1960s, replaced by a modern building in Riverside.

The official opening of the Will Adams Memorial in Gillingham in 1934. Adams, born in the town in 1564, played a key part in the early trading development of Japan.

The Adams Memorial in 1970. For many years his life was celebrated at a ceremony in Japan.

The High Street and surrounding area of Gillingham in 1970, before the pedestrianisation and other important

changes took place. St Mark's Church is in the foreground.

Some of the streets around Gillingham railway station in 1947. Gillingham still has the highest population of any

town in Kent.

The Jezreel's Tower in Canterbury Street, Gillingham in 1936. It was started, but never finished, by former soldier James White, who called himself James Jershom Jezreel and claimed to be a messenger who would build the tower up to heaven. The tower was pulled down in the early 1960s.

A typical day at Gillingham's Strand in August 1939 – still a popular recreation area today. When this picture was taken the outbreak of World War Two was only a few weeks away.

The presence of so many coaches indicates that a major function was taking place at the Central Hotel in Watling Street, Gillingham, in this 1940s picture.

Gillingham High Street in 1951.

Gillingham maintained its
independent borough status during
local government reorganisations.
The municipal buildings in
Canterbury Street housed all the
departments and the gardens have
long been a quiet resting place.

The Grand Cinema,
Gillingham, which
closed in 1960.

Rochester Castle in December 1968. It was built in Norman times and later became a very important stronghold. The huge keep dates back to the reign of Henry I.

Jasper's Gatehouse, over the entrance to Cathedral Close, provides artistic inspiration in 1970. Charles Dickens turned it into the home of opium smoker John Jasper in his unfinished novel *The Mystery of Edwin Drood*.

One road and two rail bridges crossed the River Medway at Rochester when this picture was taken in the 1950s.

The opening of the M20 bridge was some years off.

Rochester's Deanery gate in 1970.

A 1971 view of King's School, Rochester. One of the oldest public schools in England, it was founded in the seventh century and reconstituted by Henry VIII.

Dickens' association with the Medway Towns is mainly centred on Rochester, but this is the house at No.2 Ordnance Terrace in Chatham where he lived as a boy. His father, John, worked in the dockyard.

The official opening of Charles Dickens' chalet, behind Eastgate House in Rochester High Street, in 1961. It was presented to the novelist in 1864 and originally stood in the garden of Gads Hill Place at Higham, where Dickens died.

One of countless re-enactments of Dickens – now predominantly by way of the Dickens Festivals. This Dickens coach was assembled to celebrate the centenary of Cobham Cricket Club in 1950 and is seen arriving at the Bull Hotel, which figures in *Pickwick Papers*.

The 16th-century Eastgate House in 1955, later to house the Charles Dickens Centre.

Restoration House in the 1970s. It was built in the 16th century and Charles II stayed there on his way to be crowned in 1660. Dickens renamed it Satis House for *Great Expectations*. The house was later to be acquired by entertainer Rod Hull.

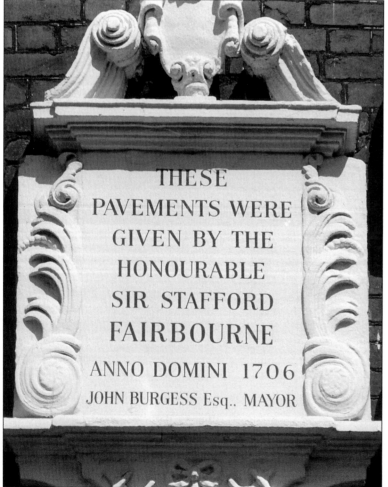

THESE PAVEMENTS WERE GIVEN BY THE HONOURABLE SIR STAFFORD FAIRBOURNE

ANNO DOMINI 1706

JOHN BURGESS Esq., MAYOR

Opposite page: Rochester Guildhall, claimed to be the finest 17th-century civic building in Kent.

One of the plaques above the Guildhall entrance.

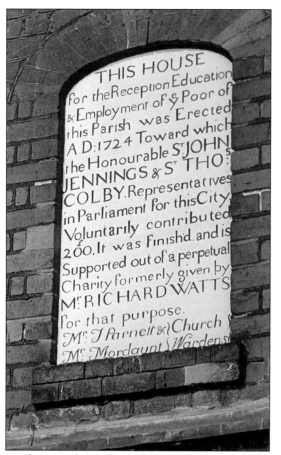

Rochester abounds with historical and civic importance, much of it marked by plaques. The Watts Charity, in the High Street, was originally founded for poor travellers to stay one night.

A 1930s picture of Foord's almshouses by the Medway at Rochester.

A Short Scion, the first aircraft to link Rochester Airport with a regular commercial service to Southend, in the summer of 1934.

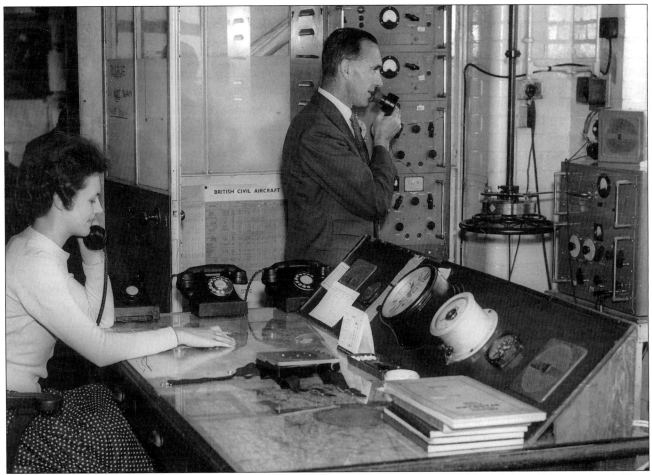

Remarkably relaxed by modern standards, this was the traffic control room at Rochester Airport in 1960.

Channel Airways operated out of Rochester in the 1960s.

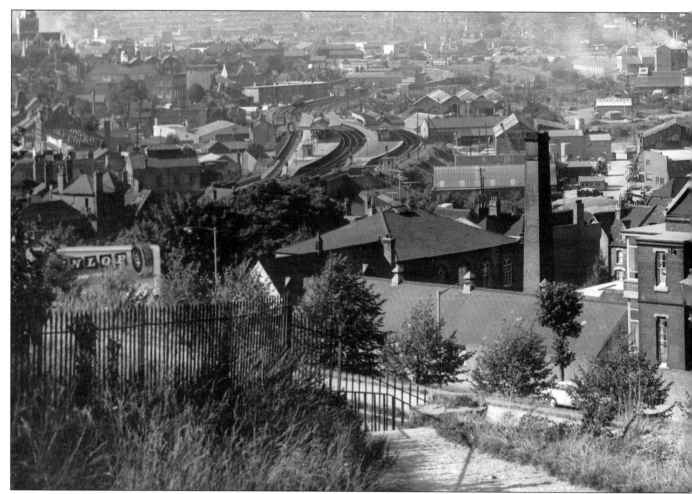

A view of St Bartholomew's Hospital, Rochester in 1961, taken from Fort Pitt.

The airport in 1969, with a rather quaint notice – and no aircraft in view.

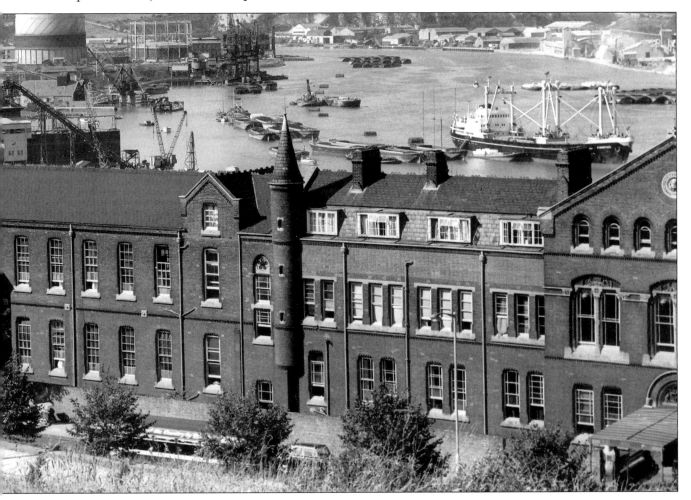

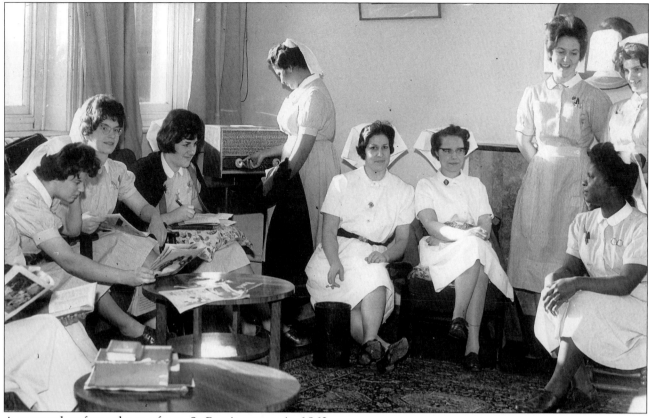

A somewhat formal pose from St Bart's nurses in 1962.

Every vehicle for itself at the foot of Star Hill, Rochester in the 1950s. They all seem to be heading for a huge pile-up.

Two views of Rochester High Street in the late 1960s, when it was beginning to suffer from the recession that eventually gave way to dedicated restoration of the city as a centre for interesting shops and tourist attractions. Before the Medway motorway bridge was built, all London and coastal-bound traffic had to crawl through the centre of Rochester.

Rochester Market, still thriving today, in 1971 just after decimal currency had been introduced. Prices were shown in old and 'new' money.

Rochester Casino, home to many forms of recreation and entertainment over the years.

Lord Cornwallis, the Lord Lieutenant of Kent, presents a Queen's Award for Export Achievements to Elliott Automation in 1971. It was the fourth year in a row that the Rochester firm had gained the award, but sadly it came at a time when 200 workers had lost their jobs because of a slump in the aircraft industry.

The industrial heartland of Strood in the 1960s.

Several former well-known high street names can be seen in this 1936 picture of Strood, but the *Kent Messenger* is still going strong.

The sign indicates that demolition had started to eradicate a traffic blackspot in Strood High Street in 1961.

The former Victorian steam roller company, Aveling and Porter, and Wingets' factory building in Strood, the site of which was to become centralised offices for Rochester-upon-Medway Council in the mid-1980s. This picture was taken 50 years before that.

The old Strood Rural District Council offices in 1970, dating back to 1934. Forty years later the authority was no longer in existence.

Rainham in the 1950s. There was a lot of development to come.

A pre-war shot of Rainham Mark.

Pupils at Rainham Council Infants' School celebrate Empire Day in May 1934. It marked the birthday of Queen Victoria.

St Margaret's Church and The Cricketers pub in Rainham High Street in 1962.

Quite a few pedal cycles are to be seen in this 1963 shot of Rainham High Street.

The days before yellow lines – Brompton High Street in 1966.

Borstal Institute in 1970. It was later renamed Medway Remand Centre. Similar penal centres for young people in other parts of the country were also called Borstals for many years.

Cobham Hall in 1970. An Elizabethan mansion designed by Inigo Jones, it became a private girls' school.

A ploughing match at Cobham in 1957.

1949 in Cobham, when the Leather Bottle like so many inns, had public and private bars. The inn features in Charles Dickens' first successful novel, *Pickwick Papers*. Notice how many people in the older picture are smoking.

Upnor Castle, built in the reign of Elizabeth I to protect the Medway and its dockyard.

Cooling Castle, now largely ruined, in 1954. It was originally the home of Sir John Oldcastle, said to be the inspiration for Shakespeare's *Falstaff*.

The post office was obviously the real centre of life in Vigo in the 1940s. Vigo was established as a wartime camp, later taken over by squatters which then developed into an orthodox village. London names were copied for many of the streets.

A 1930s shot of Burke House at Wouldham. It was once the home of Walter Burke, the purser on board HMS *Victory* – built at Chatham – who caught Admiral Nelson as he fell wounded at the Battle of Trafalgar. Nelson died in his arms.

Wouldham in 1950.

The old post office at Shorne in 1939. Charles Dickens was said to have bought his pens here.

Many of the industrial works along the Medway were the concern of environmentalists long before the word became fashionable. This was the Rugby Portland Cement works at Halling in 1962.

A 16th-century Halling house, pictured during World War Two.

Townsend Hook Paper Mills dominate this 1972 view of Snodland.

Inside the Snodland mill in 1950.

Malling Road at Snodland in 1949, long before the arrival of the by-pass. The chimneys of the cement works were demolished in 1986.

The country meets the town in this 1956 Snodland scene.

When time was not as important as today – Snodland ferry in the 1930s.

Holborough Forge at Snodland, with its unusual horseshoe doorway, in 1947.

An age of childhood innocence captured in this 1947 picture of Snodland Secondary School, later Holmesdale High.

Gad's Hill House School at Higham, one of Charles Dickens' former homes.

A 1950s shot of Blue Bell Hill, which links Maidstone with the Medway Towns and is so often misspelled Bluebell. Medway Crematorium is in the foreground. *Picture: FotoFlite, Ashford, Kent. Tel: 01233 635556.*

Traditional farming was maintained at the Isle of Grain in the mid-1950s, when the giant BP oil refinery was well into production.

The refinery in 1968, one of the biggest in the country with a capacity of millions of tons of oil a year.

Lunchtime in the BP canteen – a picture taken in 1958.

The Central Electricity Generating Board's power station at Kingsnorth, near Hoo, on the Medway. It was opened in 1968 and designed to last 40 years.

Ernest Marples, second from the left, the Minister of Transport, visited the site of the M2 motorway bridge at Rochester as it neared completion in 1962. He said it would pass "one of the worst bottlenecks on the A2".

The bridge in 1965. Traffic is seldom so light today.

Royal Visits, Civic Events, Celebrations

King George VI and Queen Elizabeth made many visits to Kent during World War Two. On 21 February 1940 the King came to Chatham and inspected members of the Women's Royal Naval service – the Wrens – at the Royal Marine Barracks.

The King was given three cheers as he left the Naval Barracks later that day.

Queen Elizabeth, later the Queen Mother, chatted to Wrens when she came to Chatham in May 1941.

The King and Queen went to Shorts factory at Rochester and were shown over some of the famous flying boats that had made such a significant contribution to the war effort. All employers later received a souvenir booklet with pictures of the visit.

The young Queen Elizabeth II and the Duke of Edinburgh went to the Isle of Grain oil refinery in April 1955, where they were received by the Lord Lieutenant of Kent, Lord Cornwallis and Lady Cornwallis.

Hundreds of employees with their wives and families cheered the royal couple at Grain. They were shown a tanker, the *British Princess*, which the Queen had launched nine years before when she was Princess Elizabeth.

The Queen made an extended visit to the Towns in October 1956. She was the first reigning monarch to call at Chatham Town Hall, where she was received by the Mayor, Alderman W.G.Rhodes.

The Mayor of Rochester, Alderman W.Wilkinson, was by the Queen's side as she walked in procession to Rochester Cathedral.

During the day the Queen made a brief visit to the cathedral. She is pictured with the Bishop, Dr C.M. Chavasse.

There was a longer visit to the cathedral in March 1961, when the Queen and Prince Phillip attended a royal Maundy service. Gifts were handed to 35 men and 35 women as the Queen was then 35. This was the scene at the west door.

As Colonel-in-Chief the Queen, with Prince Phillip, made a private visit to the Royal Engineers at Brompton barracks, Gillingham, in March 1968. One of the members of the Junior Leaders had to carry on working a few feet from Her Majesty.

An unforgettable moment as 86-year-old Sgt. H.Taylor presents a posy to the Queen at Brompton. He was among a party of Chelsea Pensioners.

The royal couple were again accompanied by Lord Cornwallis during their tour.

Princess Marina, Duchess of Kent, inspected nurses of St John Ambulance Brigade at Gillingham in 1943.

King George of Greece spoke to the three Medway mayors during his visit in 1942.

Prince George, the Duke of Kent, went to Rochester in 1931 to open the city pageant which marked 2,000 years o

its history.

One of Princess Marina's last visits to Kent was in June 1968. She arrived by helicopter at the playing field of King's School, Rochester, for the start of a busy day of engagements in the area.

Sailors parade for the birthday celebration of King George V at Chatham in June 1933.

The main gate of the dockyard being decorated for the celebration of the Silver Jubilee of King George V and Queen Mary in May 1935.

Mrs Mary Penfold, aged 101, presented jubilee mugs to children at Bredhurst village school.

The proclamation of King Edward VIII– who abdicated before being crowned – at Chatham Town Hall in January 1936.

The Vineyard public house in Rochester decorated to mark the coronation of King George VI and Queen Elizabeth in May 1937.

The following sequence illustrates events celebrating the coronation of Queen Elizabeth II in June 1953. Such orderly reverence has seldom been seen since and would be impossible today.

A fanfare at Eccles primary school.

Rene Austin is crowned Snodland's coronation Queen by Mr N. Taylor, chairman of the parish council.

The party at Richmond Road School in Gillingham.

Fancy dress entries at Birling.

The decorations at Star Hill, Rochester.

One of the main attraction at Chatham was the ox roasting organised by members of the Constitional Club.

The night scene at the dockyard gate.

Twenty-one gun salutes have frequently been fired at Chatham's naval barracks. This one, in February 1960, marked the birth of Prince Andrew.

Remembrance Day at Gillingham in 1929. It was halfway between the end of World War One and the start of World War Two.

Above: Medway Old Contemptibles – veterans of World War One – gather to remember their former colleagues in September 1935.

Right: For many years an annual Court of Admiralty was held on a barge at Rochester to agree regulations for the ancient oyster beds. This was the scene in 1952.

Below: Chatham Borough Council in session in 1968. It later became Medway and then Rochester-upon-Medway Council.

People and Events

Kent's worst road disaster occured in Dock Road, Gillingham on 4 December 1951, when a double-decker bus ploughed into Royal Marine cadets marching to a boxing tournament. Twenty-three boys were killed and 17 injured. This was the scene as marines bore the coffins to the mass grave.

The last tribute to the boys who died. They were aged between eight and 15.

Above: Police, naval and military personnel – with a large number of high-ranking officers – went to a house in Symonds Avenue, Chatham in June 1951 where Derek Poole, the 20-year-old killer of a Chatham policeman, was sheltering. When the house was entered he was found to be dead.

This narwhal, only five of which had been found off the British coast in 400 years, was washed up at Wouldham in 1949. It was later taken to the British Museum.

The severe floods of February 1953 undermined the railway line at Stoke Junction on the Isle of Grain.

The winter of 1962-63 was one of the coldest in British history. This picture was taken at Wainscott.

No more country to be seen from this particular Maidstone and District bus at High Halstow for some time. It was January 1963.

A Rochester Co-op bread van suffers in the icy conditions. Everyone looks surprisingly relaxed.

It couldn't be more formal as men go about their work in Rochester Post Office in 1938.

Medway fire station personnel staged a demonstration of their work at Gillingham in March 1957. The old Jezreel's Tower is in the background.

Pilcher's was a successful Chatham coach firm for more than 100 years. This was one of the outings it ran to the seaside in the early post-war years. Everyone seems prepared for bad weather.

The Keg Megs, which ran for more than 50 years after its launch in 1928, was a successful children's club sponsored by the *Kent Messenger*. It organised events for youngsters and raised thousands of pounds for charitable causes, particularly hospitals. This group was ready for a flight from Shorts at Rochester in 1948.

Another Keg Megs presentation. The Mayor of Rochester, Councillor Stuart Fry, hands over a television on behalf of the club at an old people's home in Balfour Road in 1965.

Hop-picking provided a combination of hard-earned extra money and holiday for thousands of people in Kent for many years before the advent of almost complete mechanisation. This smiling group was pictured at Nashenden Farm, Borstal at the start of the harvest in 1951.

Sea Rangers carried a message of goodwill across the Medway at Burham in 1950. The message ended up at the 13th world Guide conference in Oxford.

David Atkinson, Andrew Nicolson, Trevor Gransden and Paul Edwards raised money for 1st Strood Boys' Brigade in 1969 by collecting waste paper. The cash went to a fund for a campsite and training centre.

A group from a travellers' camp at Ash Tree Lane, Chatham, in the 1930s.

Political correctness was unknown when this happy group posed during Snodland Carnival celebrations in the summer of 1950.

Teachers vote to strike during a meeting of Gillingham branch of the National Union of Teachers at their centre in Gardiner Street in 1969.

British Road Services drivers marching through Strood in 1970. They had been on strike for higher wages.

Members of the Draughtsmen's and Allied Technicians' Association march to Elliott's works at Rochester in 1970 after holding a protest meeting in a local church hall.

Electioneering, 1945-style, was vastly different to today. This was the scene outside Rochester and Chatham Conservative headquarters as candidate Captain L.F.Plugge addressed passers-by. He was heavily defeated by Arthur Bottomley, who went on to become a long-standing MP, a member of the Labour cabinet and a peer.

Sir Freddie Burden, Conservative MP for Gillingham, from 1950 to 1979. Always a back-bencher, he was a noted campaigner for local causes, his last being against the closure of Chatham Dockyard. He died in 1987.

Counting the votes at the General Election in Rochester and Chatham in 1970.

Peggy Fenner, later Dame Peggy, is congratulated by her Labour opponent Anne Kerr – then the sitting Member – after winning Rochester and Chatham for the Tories in 1970.

A wonderfully-informal picture of Dr David Say (left) after his consecration as Bishop of Rochester in Canterbury Cathedral in 1961. Dr Say is with the Archbishop of Canterbury, Dr Geoffrey Fisher, and the new Bishop of Singapore. Dr Say served for 27 years and was made a Freeman of the City on his retirement.

One of the best-known businessmen in the Towns for many years, Andy Anderson was Mayor of Rochester in 1951 and 1952, during which time this picture was taken of him and his wife Alice. Mr Anderson, a freeman of the City of London, was awarded the Order of the British Empire in 1980.

The River Medway, the Dockyard, Naval and Military

Chatham Dockyard in the early 1960s, when it was still a workplace for thousands and home to hundreds of naval, military and specialist personnel.

The yard in 1970. Said to be the birthplace of the British Navy, it was built in 1558 during the reign of Elizabeth I. Two of the greatest names in naval history, Admirals Drake and Nelson, learned their sea skills there and HMS *Victory*, the greatest warship of its time, was built there and launched in 1765. After its closure as a dockyard in the 1980s it assumed new life as a centre of history, entertainment and education.

Workers in the Royal
Navy Armament
Depot at the dockyard
in 1955.

In the 1940s and '50s most
men went to work by bike.
These are on their way
home from the yard in
1946.

ALL PASSES TO
BE SHOWN

The scene had not changed much by 1960.

There were plenty of cars by 1969, but many of their drivers were prevented from entering the yard on this

occasion by a massed gathering of strikers.

One of the old naval traditions now discontinued. Sailors from Chatham's HMS *Pembroke* base enjoy their daily tot of rum in the 1940s – Splicing the Mainbrace.

HMS *Guardian*, a warship launched with due ceremony at Chatham Dockyard in 1931. It was christened by the Mayoress, Mrs H.J.Cloake.

Chatham was still building submarines well into the nuclear age. This much earlier one, HMS *Snapper*, was launched in 1934.

Dr David Say, Bishop of Rochester, officiates at the recommissioning of HMS *Chichester* at the yard in 1969.

Navy Days were a highlight of the Towns' scene in pre and post-war years. These visitors were fascinated by a submarine in 1931.

Going aboard the sub Scorcher in the 1950s.

Huge crowds at Navy Days in 1968.

Rochester River Police start their nightly beat of 20 miles up and down the Medway in 1933.

A 1950s shot of Admiral's House in the dockyard. It was built in the early 1700s.

A charming reflection of an age of innocence – the Medway at Rochester in 1953. Note the Shorts flying boat.

A thousand feet above the Medway in 1961 with industrial Strood in the foreground and Rochester with the bridge, cathedral and castle in the middle distance.

The port at Rochester in the 1960s, showing Chatham Town Hall and the naval monument on the far left.

Fishing boats mingle with houses and the church at Strood in 1970.

The winter of early 1963 was so severe that coal barges were frozen on the Medway at Rochester.

The great days of sail were still part of the everyday scene on the Medway in 1935.

The end of the day – Rochester in 1938, when red-sailed barges still plied their trade as a key feature of the Towns' industry.

A shot from June 1937 showing the variety of river craft of the time. Among them are barges preparing for their annual race.

One of the celebrated Medway pleasure steamers, the *Rochester Queen* on a blustery day in the 1940s.

The *Sidar* and its crew at Strood in 1957, by which time barges' days were numbered.

The *Medway Queen* in 1957. One of the last of a great tradition of steamers, it took part in the evacuation of British troops from Dunkirk in 1940 and later became the subject of extensive conservation efforts.

Soldiers and cadets organise trips in a D-Day assault craft from Strood pier in 1945, soon after the end of World War Two.

A peaceful scene at Upnor in 1949. The *Arethusa* was a 50-gun naval frigate that became a training ship for youngsters for many years. It was replaced by a ketch of the same name in 1975.

One of the great Medway sights of yesteryear – a Short Brothers flying boat in 1948.

Workers leave the Shorts' factory in 1936 – almost everyone is wearing a cap or a hat.

Shorts were founders of the British aviation industry and made seaplanes and flying boats at Rochester from 1913 until the bulk of its operations were transferred to Belfast in 1947. This was the amazing pre-war composit 'piggyback' *Maia* with its passenger sister *Mercury* flyir over Rochester in 1938. They set up a record flight t

...outh Africa in 1938, the mother plane flying 1,000 miles ...efore releasing *Mercury* to complete the rest of the ...000-mile journey. *Picture: Associated Press London.*

Caps were also part of the in-factory attire for most workers. This picture was taken at Shorts in 1935.

The R628, then Britain's largest flying boat, on the Medway after her first flight in July 1933.

A Short Sunderland in 1940. It was the best-known of all the Shorts craft.

Civilian forerunner of the Sunderland, a Golden Hind which could carry 150 passengers. This was part of Imperial Airways' fleet in 1939.

A huge Shorts Shetland at Rochester in 1947. It was the largest plane ever built by the firm, but only two were completed.

This was the last Solent flying boat built at Shorts in 1948. Workers gathered to mourn the end of the company's association with the Towns.

The superb band of the Royal Engineers parading at Brompton barracks in 1957.

The Royal Marines band at Chatham in 1958. Its traditions in the area already dated back 200 years.

A Gurkha piper taking part in the traditional Beating Retreat ceremony. The 69 Gurkha Independent Field Squadron had a long association with the Towns at Kitchener Barracks, Chatham.

Right: The South African arch at Brompton, pictured in the 1970s.

Left: A Royal Marine stands guard at the entrance to Melville Barracks, Chatham in 1961.

Above: Hats off – Royal Marines at Chatham celebrate the birthday of King George VI in 1936.

Brompton Barracks, where a School of Military Engineering was established in 1812.

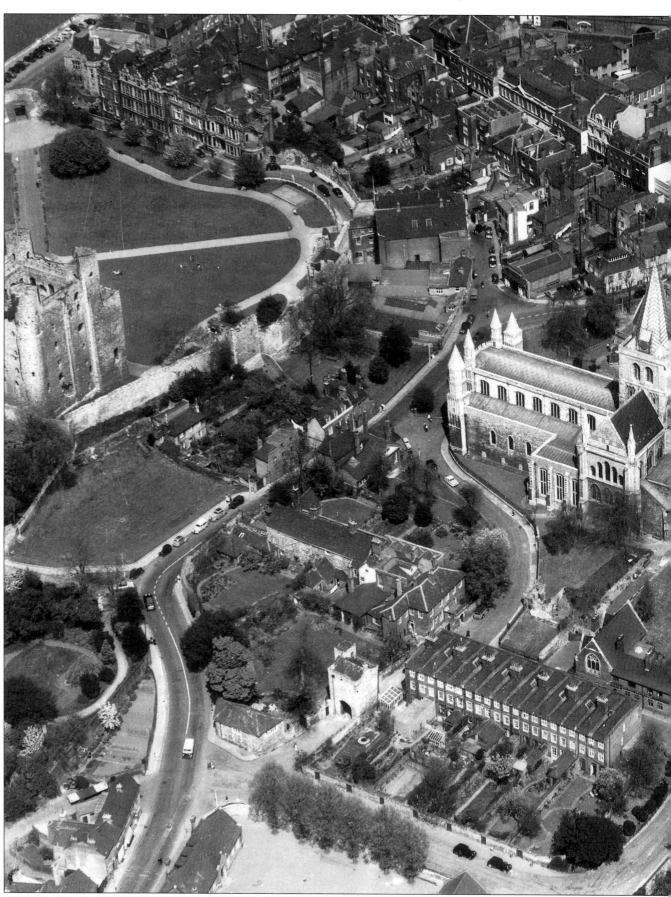

A 1958 view of Rochester Cathedral, the castle, the High Street and the market. The cathedral, the second oldest in England after Canterbury, originally dates t about 604 but was largely rebuilt by Bishop Gundulp

es and Pubs

the early 11th century. There have also been later
dditions.

Picture: Aerofilms of Borehamwood.

129

The cathedral in 1968, since when much of this western side has been beautifully cleaned.

This catalpa tree outside the cathedral was planted more than 120 years ago. It is grown from an Indian bean indigenous to North America, the West Indies and Eastern Asia.

A service in the cathedral in 1930.

The cathedral choir ready for a service at Christmas 1958.

The Dean of Rochester, the Rt Revd R.W.Stannard, and the head verger, Mr G.Stephens, hauling one of the cathedral bells into position after renovation work in time for Christmas services in 1959.

St Mary's Church in Dock Road, Chatham with Kitchener's statue prominent.

Midnight Mass at St Michael's Roman Catholic Church in Chatham at Christmas 1956.

St Paul's
Church,
Chatham.

St Mary's
Church,
Gillingham.

The new Catholic Church
at Beechings Way,
Gillingham in 1970.

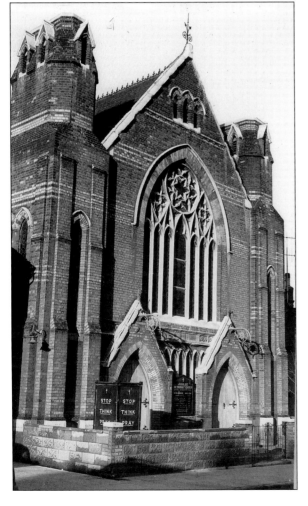

The Jubilee
Methodist Church
in Gillingham.

An old picture of Grange Chapel at Gillingham Cemetery.

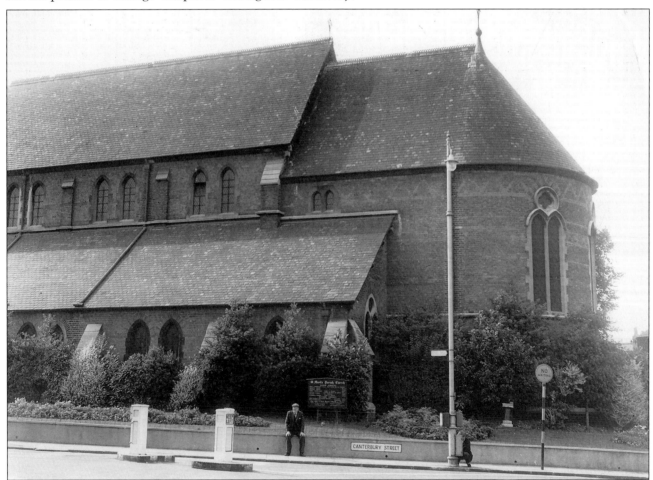

St Mark's Church, Gillingham, among the largest in the Towns.

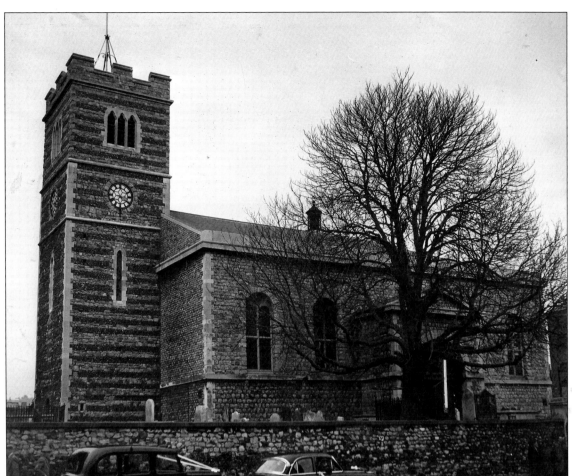

St Nicholas' Church at Strood, in 1957.

A 'new look' church – St Francis' in Strood, in 1964.

St Margaret's at Rainham.

Rainham's new Catholic Church in 1958.

The 'multi-purpose' St William's Church at Walderslade, opened in 1973.

A 1940s ceremony of blessing the plough at Shorne Parish Church.

Hoo Parish Church.

A village ceremony at Burham in 1956.

The church at Allhallows in 1956.

Restoration was
carried out at
Snodland Church in
1955.

Birling Church
in 1965.

St Peter's Church at Stoke on the Isle of Grain.

A beautiful shot of Luddesdown Church in 1960.

Most of the following sequence is of pubs, inns and eating houses that have long since been pulled down, undergone name changes or been altered beyond recognition. Many of the pictures were taken in the 1930s, '40s and '50s.

The Old Iron Ship at Gillingham.

The Prince of Wales in Gillingham.

The Westcourt Arms Hotel in Gillingham.

The Coopers Arms in
Rochester. This was one
of the oldest pubs in the
country. Monks, attached
to the cathedral, made
barrels of wine – hence
the name.

The King's Head
Hotel in Rochester.

The Red Lion in
Rochester.

The Morden Arms
in Rochester.

The White
Hart in
Chatham.

The Halfway
House in Chatham.

The Naval and
Military Arms in
Chatham.

The Army and
Navy Hotel in
Chatham.

The Ropemakers Arms in Chatham.

The World's End in Chatham.

The Gibraltar
Hotel in
Chatham.

The Lord Duncan in
Chatham.

The Hen & Chickens at Luton.

The Queen's Head at Wigmore.

The Flying Saucer at Hempstead. This was the opening ceremony.

The Pelican at Strood.

The Golden Lion at Luddesdown.

The Who'd Ha' Thought It at Wouldham.

The Robin Hood at Blue Bell Hill.

The Upper Bell at Blue Bell Hill.

The Three
Crutches at
Frindsbury.

The Rose
and
Crown at
Shorne.

The Towns at War

One of the workers at the West Door of Rochester Cathedral amused passers-by with his antics as security sandbags were piled up in 1939. No one knew at the time that this was to be the period of The Phoney War and that air raids were some time away.

3 September 1939 marked the outbreak of World War Two. Within days precautions were taken to guard buildings against enemy air attacks. This was Chatham Town Hall in the first week of the war.

Auxiliary firemen carry out drill at Rochester Esplanade in 1939.

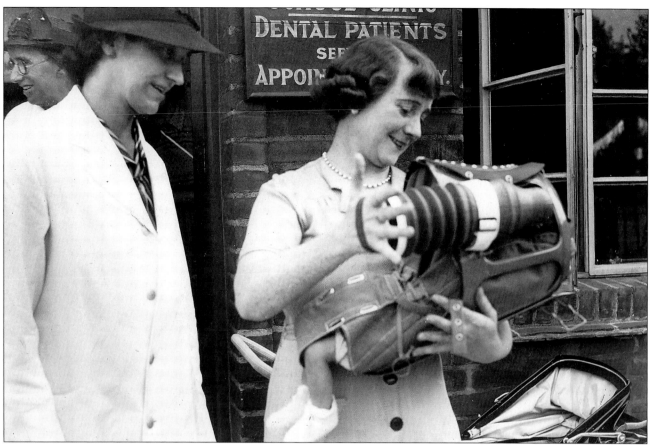

This Gillingham mother appears remarkably relaxed as she fits her baby into one of the monstrous special anti-gas bags.

The Royal Navy was ready for emergencies immediately war began. These men at Chatham are making arrangements to have some of their pay sent home to their families.

These little girls at Chatham railway station were among the first to be evacuated from their homes to areas considered to be safe from the threat of bombing.

Boys from the King's School in Rochester spent the early part of the war in Scotney Castle at Lamberhurst in Kent.

Mr R.H.Ellis, of Shakespeare Road, Gillingham, named his garden air-raid shelter Chocolate Hill after the more official one he had helped construct at Gallipoli during World War One.

This Chatham man pauses to admire the shelter he built to protect himself and his family – one of thousands all over the country.

Anxious parents prepare to say goodbye to their children being evacuated from Gillingham.

Men were soon being called up for service in the armed forces. This was registration time for the 20-25 age group at Chatham Labour Exchange in April 1940.

Queues were many but orderly. This was the long wait for oranges and lemons at Chatham early in the war.

Good humour marked everyday activities before the war took a turn for the worse. This was the scene as shutters went up to protect windows of the Royal Exchange Hotel, Chatham.

Nearly everyone joined in the war effort. This picture of Air Raid Precaution wardens was taken at Chatham on Boxing Day 1939.

Cycle power kept ARP members mobile most of the time. Here, Lord Knollys visited a parade at Gillingham in April 1941.

Men from the National Fire Service station at Ordnance Street, Chatham, were inspected by Mr B.A.Westbrook, of the Home Offfice, in 1940.

Girl soldiers march to their duties at an anti-aircraft gun battery at Fort Horsted in 1942.

A Green Line bus was converted into use as an ambulance to transfer patients to and from St Batholomew's Hospital, Rochester.

Barrage baloons were a common sight over Kent as a means of peventing raids from low-flying German aircraft. This one was positioned near oast houses at Cobham.

An emergency bridge was built by Army personnel across the River Medway at Wouldham. The picture was censored at the time.

National Fire Service despatch rider Miss P.G.Greason hands a message to local commander G.H.Robinson at Chatham.

Hundreds of people had to leave their homes after the bombing. Here ARP workers are helping out at Wickham Street.

Once the German bombing began, large areas of the Medway Towns suffered severe damage. This was the carnage at Wickham Street, Delce, Rochester in April 1941.

A mother and her young child were among the victims of this attack on Temple Farm Estate, Strood in February 1944.

The dreadful task of clearing up after bombs fell on Station Road, Strood in 1944.

The first flying bombs – VIs or Doodle Bugs – fell in the summer of 1944. This devastation was caused at Snodland.

Civilians, servicemen and emergency service members at the scene of more flying bomb damage in Grafton Avenue, Rochester in November 1944.

The BBC broadcast one of its *Works Wonders* lunchtime variety shows from Shorts' canteen at Rochester in January 1944.

These workers, also at Rochester, joined in with popular entertainer Gracie Fields during one of her many visits to Kent in the war years.

Above: Marches and ceremonial events kept morale high during the war. This group of Wrens – the Women's Royal Naval Service – was inspected by Queen Elizabeth at Chatham in May 1941.

Below: The Mayor of Rochester, Councillor. C.S.Knight, takes the salute at a march past of Home Guards in 1941 – and a little girl joins in.

The band of the Royal Marines led a massed procession through Chatham to mark Warship Week in 1942. It was one of many such weeks held to raise money for a particular cause.

Rear Admiral A.G.Kirk, of the United States Navy, inspected the King's Squad of the Royal Marines at Chatham Barracks in December 1942.

A proud moment for Marine G.Cordon-Gilbert as he receives the King's Badge from Lt. General T.L.Hunter at Chatham in March 1943.

Wings for Victory Week in 1943 was the reason for this huge gathering for a drumhead service at the United Services Sports Ground at Gillingham.

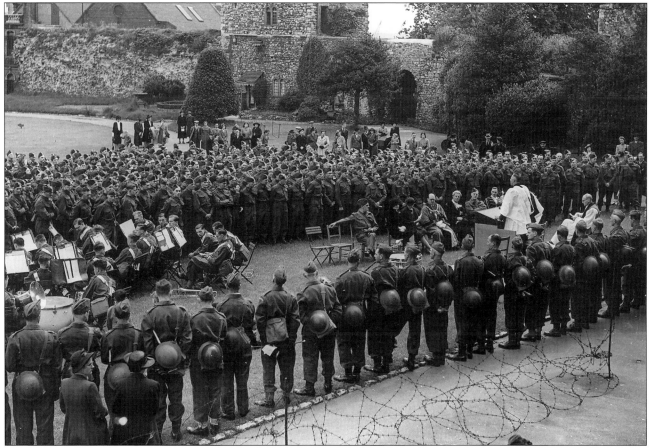

Members of Medway Home Guard paraded at Strood and then went to Rochester Castle gardens for a drumhead service conducted by the Revd L.D.James, senior chaplain of the forces.

Men who were too young for call-up served in the Home Guard. This was the 1st Kent Cadet Batallion at their inspection by General Sir H.E.Franklyn at Chatham in March 1944.

Signalman Len Bowley spent four years as a prisoner of the Germans after HMS *Gloucester* was sunk off Crete in 1941. This was the happy scene at his home in Wilson Avenue, Rochester as the war ended in 1945.

Sport and Recreation

No one staged protest demonstrations when the the Royal Engineers Hunt moved off from Meopham in November 1934.

The *Kent Messenger* organised Old Crocks Runs for veteran cars through Kent in the early 1930s.

This one finished at Rochester Guildhall where one of the winners, Mr F.S.Rowden, in an 1898 Sta

Dog Cart, is being greeted by the Mayor, Councillor G.Jenner, and Mr H.R.Pratt Boorman, editor-proprietor of the *Kent Messenger*.

The finals of the *Kent Messenger* county darts competition in the Pavilion, Gillingham, in 1935, with winning captain H.Waghorn, of The Bull's Head, Dartford, enjoying the first drink from the trophy.

Cricket at Meopham Green in 1956 – a much-photographed scene that survives virtually unchanged today. Meopham may not be generally associated with the Towns, but it was once within the Strood Rural District Council area.

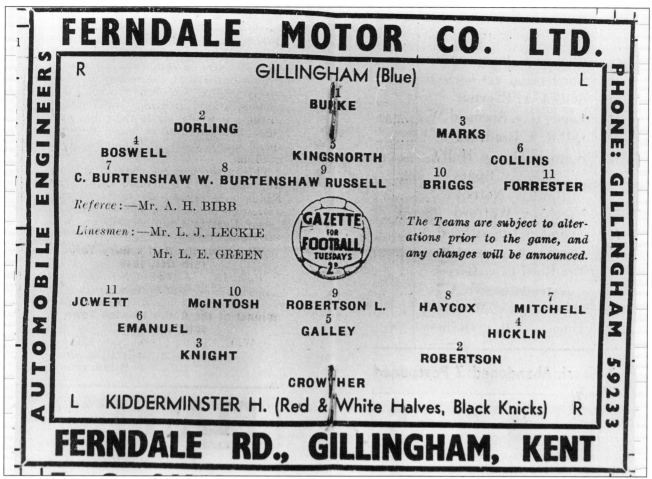

The leading sports club in the Medway Towns, Gillingham FC have experienced widely-fluctuating fortunes. This was a programme from 1949-50, their last season in the Southern League before regaining the Football League place they lost just before World War Two. 'Black knicks' seem curious by today's standards.

No play today – snow clearing in vain from Gillingham's Priestfield Stadium pitch during the bad winter of 1962-63. The man in the tracksuit is manager Freddie Cox who, the following season piloted the club to promotion from the Fourth Division.

Chatham Town have fielded a senior soccer team for many seasons. This was their line-up for an Aetolian League game in September 1961. Player-manager Don Rossiter (seated second left) later became a prominent Rochester councillor.

Above: Gillingham's Third Division squad of 1970-71, with manager Basil Hayward (back row, extreme left) and long-serving chairman Dr Clifford Grossmark (seated second right).

Chatham's Mickey Walker became one of the leading woman golfers in Britain while still a teenager in the early 1970s. She was the youngest player this century to win the English Ladies' Open championship.

So Many Stunning Changes

IF A MEDWAY man emigrated to Australia in 1980 and returned home today for the first time, he would be stunned by the changes.

Firstly he would not even recognise the road layout as he drove up the A229 into Chatham and, never before encountering the town's ring road system, would probably get lost in it.

He would discover for the first time that the River Medway had a road tunnel and that three bridges crossing the river at Cuxton instead of one.

He would find familiar landmarks such as Rochester's tower blocks gone and would come across entirely new places such as the Splashes Leisure Pool in Rainham and Gillingham Ice Bowl.

Such has been the massive changes to the area in the last quarter century.

Major historical events have themselves shaped and affected the Medway Towns.

The last couple of decades have been marked by the Falklands War of 1982, the 1991 Gulf conflict, the Great Storm of 1987 and, one of the most tragic recent events, the 1998 Kent Air Ambulance crash.

But the area's single most far-reaching event was the closure of Chatham Dockyard in 1984.

Medway's economy was brought to its knees, with a loss of 8,000 jobs, and most families in the area were affected.

To bring Medway back on its feet the redundant land at Chatham Maritime was redeveloped and the area's road networks improved to attract business.

Just about none of the dockyard land today is recognisable save for the old buildings preserved in The Historic Dockyard. The rest of the area has been transformed for new business and homes.

Many of the changes have had to be forced on by progress. The mass of new roads have had to be built to accommodate the increase of car use and the demands for better infrastructure for business and the economy. The days when traffic to London used to pass straight through Rochester and Chatham High Streets are long gone, and with wider motorways and more and more bypasses journeys become quicker, at least in theory.

The demolition of tower blocks, particularly during the 1980s, symbolises changes in how we want to live.

These high-rise flats, the planners' dream of the 1960s, became a tenants' nightmare with broken-down lifts and vandals setting fire to rubbish chutes.

To tenants they were prisons in the sky with residents feeling trapped and isolated – nobody wanted to live in them, so they had to go.

With so many changes in the last 25 years who knows what the next 25 will bring?

The 10-storey Fairborne House tower block in The Tideway, Rochester, before its demolition and on the day it came down in September 1981. The block, nicknamed Faulty Tower, caused one last headache when a whole section was left intact after the blast. Tower blocks became the tenant's nightmare because of poor living conditions and many were demolished during the Eighties.

Six-year-old Jamie Seton pushed the button to trigger the demolition blast for Fairborne House in Rochester, watched by thousands. Jamie, of Horsted Way, Chatham, got this chance when he won first prize in a raffle.

Rochester High Street was being restyled in 1981 to its present touristy/Dickens era look. Pictured are workmen resurfacing the road.

Gillingham's Television Theatre in Duncan Road in 1982. The former Plaza cinema, had been used to make programmes such as the *Muppets* spin-off *Fraggle Rock*. But bosses at TVS (Meridian's predecessor) announced its closure in 1987 and work was moved to larger studios in Maidstone.

This sign in on the A2 Chatham/Gillingham boundary in 1984 provoked complaints from locals. It replaced a sign simply saying 'Chatham' and people said it made visitors think they were driving straight into Rochester.

The closed Rochester Odeon in the High Street near Star Hill, 1984. Plans to turn it into a bingo hall flopped. The game was in decline then, although there was a revival of fortunes in the 1990s.

The construction of Gillingham ice Bowl in 1984. The £1 million complex at Gillingham Business park was designed to cater for 1,200 skaters and former Olympic gold medallist Robin Cousins was appointed director of coaching.

Three glamorous TV stars were brought in to help push the sale of Mountbatten House in 1985. The Chatham skyscraper had remained empty in the 11 years since its completion and Fiona Fullerton, Anneka Rice and Diane Keane (left to right) had been drafted in to promote it to businesses.

Dr Suja Hafiz is pictured with another healthy newborn baby at All Saints' Hospital, Chatham, in 1985. The hospital was a main birthplace for the town's children, with its own special care baby unit, right until the end of the century.

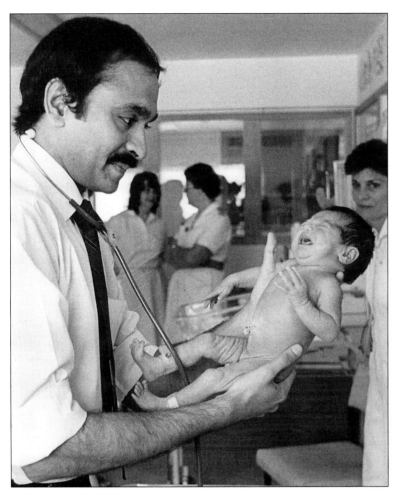

A 1993 picture of All Saints' Hospital in Magpie Hall Road, Chatham. By 1999 services had merged at Medway Hospital in Gillingham, renamed Medway Maritime. All Saints' was demolished and replaced by housing.

Good riddance was the cry from onlookers when these two tower blocks crashed to the ground in September 1986. Queen and Morden courts, near Rochester Police Station, became hated like other tower blocks. Tenants saw them as high rise prisons and there were regular problems such as broken down lifts and feelings of isolation.

The opening ceremony for the Civic Centre in Strood, October 1986. Pictured are Rochester upon Medway City Council chief executive Richard Painter, left, and council leader Doug MacInnes. The project was £5.5 million and the centralised offices became a nerve centre for the running of Strood, Chatham and Rochester.

The building of the Sir John Hawkins Flyover, 1987. The scheme was part of the Chatham Ring Road, completed in 1989, to ease traffic congestion in the town.

Development company bosses survey a scale model for the redevelopment of Chatham Maritime in 1988. The development was estimated at £600 million and planners were sensitive to the views of Prince Charles who was making scathing attacks on some of Britain's architecture at the time.

This was the devastation caused when a 17-ton caterpillar track slid off a lorry in Gillingham High Street in August 1987. It shattered paving stones and sent one hurtling through this shop window, narrowly missing an elderly customer.

St Justus Church in Rochester was totally wrecked by the Great Storm of October 16, 1987. Workmen are pictured carrying away the broken cross.

St Justus Church, Rochester, was completely flattened by the Great Storm of 1987.

The Great Storm of 1987 caused utter devastation throughout Southern England and wrecked several homes. The storm peeled away a whole section of this house in Coulman Street, Gillingham. Note the exposed upper bedroom with the rear double wardrobe exposed.

Tents are flattened at this circus in Jacksons Field, Rochester, during the Great Storm of 1987.

Another horrendous result of the Great Storm of 1987. A huge tree is uprooted and collapses on the home of retired head teacher Jon Boad, in Chicago Avenue, Gillingham.

Parts of Walderslade looked like a jungle after the 1987 Great Storm, with fallen trees and foliage. But this milkman still battled through to make his deliveries.

The releasing of balloons for the 10th anniversary of Hempstead Valley Shopping Centre, Gillingham, in 1988.

A landmark birthday for Hempstead Valley Shopping Centre. Dai Liyanage, Medway Mayor at the turn of the century, blows out the candles for the 21st birthday cake in 1999.

In 1989 villagers at Halling, Wouldham and Burham united to fight British Rail plans to let the Channel Tunnel Rail Link pass their area. Pupils from Halling primary school spelt out their response to the plans in this aerial picture.

Youngsters at Halling in 1989 made clear their opposition to the Channel Tunnel Rail Link proposals. Both Routes 1 and 2, although coming from different parts of London, would affect their area.

One of the youngest protesters in 1989 against the Channel Tunnel Rail Link in the Halling area.

A canine protester against the Channel Tunnel Rail Link route, which was planned to pass near Burham, Wouldham and Halling, 1989.

Burham people in 1989 protest against the planned Channel Tunnel Rail Link route, which would run south of their village.

Medway's biggest secondary school suffered a massive fire in 1989. The blaze at The Howard School in Rainham ironically broke out less than two hours after a fire drill and the second alarm sounding was at first thought to be another practice.

Long queues outside the Cannon Cinema in Chatham High Street were once typical, as this 1989 photograph shows. The cinema, at the corner of Upbury Way, became the ABC by the 1990s but the lure of modern multiplexes sealed its fate. When it closed 2002 only 69 people turned up to see the last film, despite it being the blockbuster *Lord of the Rings*.

This 1986 picture shows work progressing on the dualling of the A2 New Road in Chatham and the reconstruction of the Luton Arches roundabout. It was completed in 1990. Note the building of the New Road footbridge and the traffic island roundabout.

Traffic seems to be on collision course in this 1980 picture of Luton Arches The area, a junction of five roads, had been Medway's equivalent to Piccadilly Circus with a big city accident rate to match. The problem was eventually tackled with one-way routes, a new roundabout and the dualling of the A2 New Road, all completed by 1990.

Houses in New Road, Chatham, being demolished in 1989 to make way for the dualling of the road, completed the following year.

The A2 New Road, Chatham, near Luton Arches in January 1980, 10 years before the road was dualled. Houses pictured on the left were demolished to make way for the new road layout.

Splashes Leisure Pool in Bloors Lane, Rainham, which opened in May 1990.

Rainham Station, 1990, with its modern look. Trains and stations were continually upgraded but some things never changed – fares were still considered too high and trains overcrowded.

205

The building of the Stirling sports centre in Maidstone Road, Rochester, February 1991. The opening ceremony took place in December of the following year.

The Colonial and Mutual Headquarters overlooking the former Chatham Dockyard basin in the Chatham Maritime development there. The building is pictured in 1992 when it won a regional award for the quality of its brickwork.

For years there have been complaints about the eastern end of Chatham High Street becoming more and more run down. Note the reasonable condition of these three businesses in 1992 and below the state they ended up in, in 1999.

Chatham's former post office in Railway Street in 1994. By the next decade it was closed and turned into a pub fittingly called the Old Post Office.

The Princess Royal opened the £80 million Medway Tunnel on June 12, 1996. This, the third road crossing across the river at Medway, was hoped to ease traffic congestion in the area. With the associated Wainscott Northern Bypass and Gillingham Northern Link it was also hoped to help in the area's economic regeneration.

This July 1996 picture shows the Bridgewood Roundabout in Chatham, transformed beyond recognition by the A2/M2 widening project less than five years later. The white hangar-like building in the upper centre of the photo shows the Asda superstore still being built.

Veronica Norman became the first customer of the Asda store in Chatham. She is pictured on the opening day on December 2, 1996 with her prizewinning bottle of champagne.

An aerial view of Chatham, 1997, showing the changes over the previous 20 years. It includes the Pentagon Shopping Centre, opened in 1975 and Mountbatten House, built in 1974. Behind the office block is the Sir John Hawkins flyover, opened as part of the new Chatham ring road in 1989. On the other side of The Brook, to the right of the small service flyover road, is Medway Magistrates Court, opened in 1979.

Two soldiers walk through the main arch of the parade ground at Brompton Barracks, Gillingham, in 1998. At the time the barracks were threatened with closure and a local Save Our Sappers campaign was launched.

The new Medway Council unitary authority came into being on April 1, 1998, replacing the old Rochester upon Medway and Gillingham district councils. Here Dr Richard Simmons, new council's director of planning and transport, helps workmen put up a new road sign reflecting the change.

Medway Secure Training Centre, Britain's first privately run children's jail, was wracked with controversy after its opening in April 1998. The centre, in Sir Evelyn Road, Rochester, had 14 major disturbances in its first year including a major riot in June. It was also slammed as the 'Medway Hilton' for the 'cushy' conditions for its 70 12 to 14-year-old inmates with landscaped gardens, en-suite showers and private telephone lines.

The director and staff at Medway Secure Training Centre at its opening in April 1998. A few years later it would be surprising if any of these people were still there. Two-thirds of the 100 staff, a number of whom suffered assaults, walked out in the first two years.

The derelict East End pub, Chatham High Street, 1991.

Medway joined the worldwide celebrations for the new Millennium on New Year's Eve 1999. Pictured are Sarah, Simon and Emma Beckford who turned up to see the lighting of the Millennium Beacon at the riverside in Strood.

Another New Year 2000 celebration, Frances Dukeson and Neil Cheesman at Dashmonden Close, Wainscott.

Street parties were held throughout Medway to see in the new Millennium. Pictured, from left, are Kieran Delves, Ray Male and Mick Weston at Smith Road, Lordswood.

Laura Belcher and Jodie Johnson at the Millennium street party in Smith Road, Lordswood.

Peter Stock and Matt Fisher at the Millennium street party at Glenwood Close, Hempstead. The soundtrack of the 20th century was played at that party with music from George Formby and Vera Lynn to Oasis and the Spice Girls.

Samantha Ellis and Robin Martin, of Medway Youth Parliament with the award-winning Millennium Arches sculpture at Victoria Gardens, Chatham, 1999. The arches were later smashed down by vandals.

A new annual music festival called Parklife began in Gillingham Park during the time of Britpop, the 1990s explosion of successful British rock bands. The event was named after Blur's 1994 landmark album. Pictured are the all-girl group And Why Not in 2000.

Three-year-old Jasper Craib at Diggerland. The unique adventure park opened at the Medway City Estate in Strood in 2000 and became a world first in giving children the opportunity to handle real JCB earthmoving equipment under supervision.

Gillingham FC fans celebrating the team's win into Division One at the Wembley Stadium play-offs in 2000. It was second time lucky as the team had narrowly lost at Wembley the year before.

A huge crowd gathers in Gillingham Park to greet the victorious Gillingham FC players on their victory parade after reaching Division One in the Wembley play offs in 2000. The team arrived in an open top London double decker and the parade ended at the Municipal Buildings.

Where there was once a single bridge crossing the River Medway at Cuxton, by the 21st century there were three. The 1963-built M2 bridge was joined by a second carrying traffic in the other direction and the Channel Tunnel Rail Link Bridge, as this 2000 picture shows.

By the turn of the century computers in schools were as familiar a sight as blackboards and chalk once were. This 2001 picture shows Medway Council director of education Rose Collinson with sixth formers in Robert Napier School in Gillingham.

This 2001 picture shows some of the luxury waterfront homes at St Mary's Island, part of the massive redevelopment of Chatham Maritime following the closure of Chatham Dockyard in 1984.

This 2002 photo shows a depressingly regular sight on the A228 on the Hoo Peninsula - a lorry tumbled into one of the road's many treacherous ditches. This became one of Medway's most dangerous roads with 28 deaths between 1984 and 2003.

Campaigners fought hard for safety improvements on the killer A228, as this 2000 picture shows. The Medway Messenger and its predecessor Medway Today launched safety campaigns and Medway Council raised money for the road's dualling.

From the year 2000 a massive project went under way to widen the A2 and M2 between Gillingham and Cobham. This 2002 picture shows the progress over the River Medway. The original 1960s M2 bridge was joined by a second motorway bridge carrying traffic in the other direction and a Channel Tunnel Rail Link bridge.

A 1981 picture of the old Featherstones store in Rochester High Street.

Chatham's Gala bingo hall suffered doubled disaster in 1998. First it was ravaged by a huge fire in September, then the scaffolding subsequently put up collapsed in November. These dramatic scenes show a firefighter on a high ladder tackling the billowing flames.

Chatham High Street is carpeted by the debris of collapsed scaffolding around the Gala bingo hall, November 1998. The scaffolding had been put up after the building had been struck by fire two months earlier.

July 26, 1998 – one of the blackest days in Medway's recent history. The Rochester-based Kent Air Ambulance crashed near Burham. Pilot Graham Budden and paramedics Tony Richardson and Mark Darby died instantly. Here crash investigators continue their examination of the wreckage on the following day.

On July 26, 1998 the three-man crew of the Kent Air Ambulance were killed when their helicopter crashed near Burham. This picture shows the floral tributes at the KAA base at Rochester Airport.

Chatham Dockyard workers' representatives arrive in Parliament in June 1981 to plea for the saving of the yard. Only days earlier Medway had received a body blow by Defence Secretary John Nott's announcement that it would close. Unions and workers battled in vain for three years to save the yard but it shut in 1984.

The flag at Chatham Dockyard is lowered for the last time before its 1984 closure, ending 400 years of links between the Medway towns and the Royal Navy. The closure cost 8,000 jobs and was expected to take £39 million out of the economy.

The Queen visited Medway on March 28, 2002 to celebrate the new Universities at Medway partnership between the University of Kent and University of Greenwich. Both had sites in Chatham Maritime and the area at the time of writing is seeing a uni-explosion with an new campus being built, which is expected to lead to a combined student population of 10,000. This photograph shows part of the crowd which greeted Her Majesty.

These anti-war demonstrators were heckled and called traitors by bystanders as they marched through Rochester and Chatham in February 1991. The protest was against Britain's first Gulf War against Saddam Hussein and, as often in a conflict, opinion was divided over whether the fighting was justified.

The funeral of the first Kent soldier killed during the 1991 Gulf War. Royal Engineer Lt Col Alec Wright, 49, was honoured with a 12-gun salute at the Fort Pitt military cemetery in City Way, Rochester. The service was at the Garrison Church in Brompton.

Chatham Dockyard, although doomed to closure, saw a sudden frenzy of activity during the 1982 Falklands Conflict as ships were prepared for action. Vessels that did not go directly to the South Atlantic were used to fill in gaps left in other areas of service. Here a bugler salutes one of the ships taken out of mothballs, HMS *Falmouth*.